Blessings!
—

BIBLICALLY RESPONSIBLE INVESTING

About The Author

Robert Netzly is a frequent guest and contributor on FOX Business, The New York Times, The Wall Street Journal, The Huffington Post, The Financial Times, Bloomberg and other major media for his expertise on biblically responsible investing.

He is also the Founder and CEO of the Inspire Impact Group, the parent company of leading faith-based financial firms such as Inspire Investing, Christian Wealth Management and inspireinsight.com.

Robert lives in a small agricultural community on the fringe of the Silicon Valley with his astoundingly amazing wife of 15 years, Lisa, and their four incredibly sensational children, who they enthusiastically homeschool.

Robert also helps teach Sunday school (along with Lisa), facilitates a midweek community group and helps lead the men's ministry at his home church, Grace Bible.

To read more from Robert Netzly, visit his blog at www.inspireinvesting.com.

BIBLICALLY RESPONSIBLE INVESTING

For God's Glory And
Your Joy

Robert Netzly

Inspire Press

BIBLICALLY RESPONSIBLE INVESTING ©
copyright 2018 by Robert Netzly.

All rights reserved. No part of this book may be reproduced in any form whatsoever, by photography or xerography or by any other means, by broadcast or transmission, by translation into any kind of language, nor by recording electronically or otherwise, without permission in writing from the author, except by a reviewer, who may quote brief passages in critical articles or reviews.

ISBN: 978-0-692-03967-0

Printed in the United States of America

First printing: 2018

Inspire Press
650 San Benito St, Ste. 130
Hollister, CA 95023 (USA)

For Lisa.
I couldn't do it without you, beautiful.

CONTENTS

Introduction	1
Biblically Responsible Investing Ruined My Life	5
Inspired	11
Whatever You Do	21
God's Word On Investing	31
Did God Really Say?	39
Saving Babies	43
Christian Loser Weirdo	49
Does Your Conscience Have A Price?	61
Dear Rich People	71
Risky Business	83
Bitcoin Binge: To Byte Or Not To Byte?	91
Start	99
APPENDIX - Critical Considerations When Looking For A Christian Financial Advisor	107

Acknowledgements

Much of this book is the story of God working in my life, which He often does through the people He puts into my life, and I am so thankful for each of them. There are too many people for me to acknowledge properly, but I will name a few:

To my amazing team at Inspire. You guys are such a blessing to me, each and every day. That I get to work with such a Christ-loving and fun-loving group of people means so much to me. Thank you for your passion for our mission and the movement. Together we are inspiring transformation for God's glory throughout the world!

Joe, Michael and Robby, thank you for trusting God, and believing in me, enough to join that crazy Christian startup and help start something truly amazing.

Aaron, thank you for keeping us ship shape and being my trusted right hand.

To Eric Dunavant, your steadfast support and invaluable friendship are a true blessing from God.

To my brothers and sisters of Christian Wealth Management, thank you for your enthusiasm to advance the biblically responsible investing movement.

To Bob and Rachel Barber, thank you for lending me and Lisa your Expedition. And thank you for helping me make that first step into the BRI world.

To everybody who has been there for me, encouraging me, plowing the field in front of me: I thank God for you in my life. Thank you.

Introduction

This could be a dangerous book for you. I really mean that.

Within these pages is the story of how my life was turned upside down by my discovery of something called biblically responsible investing (BRI), how the Holy Spirit pierced my heart about this issue and my rather harrowing experience of leaving everything to follow Jesus into an uncertain future with no safety net.

And the same thing could happen to you. In fact, I would love it if it did. In fact, I am praying that you would have your own version of my experience, because I cannot imagine my life without it.

Danger is not always a bad thing, it turns out.

Also within these pages is the story of how God is on the move in the financial industry, and the very real, very powerful biblically responsible investing movement underway. Christians across the globe are investing billions of dollars in alignment with biblical values for God's glory and their joy. And as they do so, their hearts are being drawn nearer to the heart of God, their worship is becoming more rich, their satisfaction in Christ is becoming more complete and their lives are shining more brightly for God's glory.

I know this because I have connected with thousands of Christian investors and I have seen it first-hand. And I know because this is what is happening in my own life, too. Jesus taught us, "Where your treasure is, there your heart will be also" (Matthew 6:21), and it is true.

Not only that, but the BRI movement is altering the fabric of Wall Street so that biblical values are being taken notice of by the corporate executives of some of the largest companies in the world.

In this book I share about exciting success stories that we have had by the grace of God, influencing some of the biggest corporations in America to respect biblical values in their corporate policies, products and philanthropic practices. We have seen major corporations end their financial support of Planned Parenthood, global hotel chains remove adult entertainment from their properties, and other encouraging victories. All because Christians chose to align their investments with biblical values and let the companies they invest in know about it.

Also in these pages are a carefully curated collection of thoughts and reflections I have had over the past several years as God has plunged me headfirst into this biblically responsible investing movement that is literally changing the way Christians invest all over the world for the glory of God.

My prayer is that, in reading this book, your heart would be drawn closer to God and that you would see Him more glorious and that you would be more fully equipped to "whether you eat or drink, or whatever you do, do all to the glory of God" (1 Corinthians 10:31).

Sure, this is a book about investing. But really it is a book about the connection between your investments, God's glory and your joy. May grace and peace be yours in abundance as you explore the imperative joy that comes of honoring God with your investment decisions.

Blessings!

Chapter 1

Biblically Responsible Investing Ruined My Life

I Had It All

I had it all: a healthy salary with healthy bonuses; job security in the "private client" division of one of the largest and most prestigious banks in the nation; a fancy office in a community dripping with wealth (and a view of the Pacific Ocean out the second floor window); an easy commute down beautiful Highway 1 on the coast of California…life was good.

And then I stumbled upon the concept of biblically responsible investing (BRI), and it ruined my life for the better.

Discovering Biblically Responsible Investing

I wasn't looking for information on biblically responsible investing, just searching for a Bible study to teach at my church on the subject of finances. But there I was, sitting at my desk, reading an article that Google decided to put on my screen about paying attention to not just the financial aspect of an investment portfolio, but the moral aspect of an investment portfolio – with biblical morals as the compass.

I had heard of socially responsible investing (SRI), which I associated with a rather narrow view of issues managed from a progressive liberal viewpoint. Being a Bible-believing Christian, such an approach did not resonate with my values and I never gave it much attention.

But, it had never crossed my mind to consider the moral implications of investment decisions from a biblical perspective, and my curiosity was piqued.

Conviction

Curious as I was, I began looking into my portfolio and the portfolios of my clients, and immediately the Holy Spirit gripped my heart and I was stunned with a conviction I was not expecting to find.

Here I was, the president of our local pro-life pregnancy center, while at the same time owning three stocks of companies that were manufacturing abortion drugs. It struck me that every time a young lady walked into the Planned Parenthood across the street and had an abortion, I was making money on that transaction.

With God's money, no less.

Quickly the Spirit reminded me that I was going to stand before my Lord Jesus one day and give an account for every word, thought, deed – and yes, every investment – in my life, and I could not imagine the conversation going very well when it came to my portfolio.

Me: "Look at all the money I made for you by investing in abortion, Jesus! Aren't you proud?"

Jesus: "No, not really."

And not just abortion, but pornography, human trafficking, LGBT activism, and all manner of unholiness festered in my investment lineup like some "Hottest Stock Picks" newsletter from hell.

Within days I was dead in the water at my dream job, completely unable to function with a clean conscience. And I had no idea what to do about it.

Drop Your Nets And Follow Me

I went home and told my wife what I had found, "Hunny, I think the Lord is calling us somewhere else."

Her response: "Okay…you know we have two babies and a mortgage, so what's the plan?"

Me: "I have no idea. I think we should pray."

I really didn't think I could stay in the investment business. I had never met or heard of anyone investing according to biblical values, and I wasn't sure it was even possible to do. I was very close to just throwing in the towel on investment advice, going to seminary and being a pastor.

The only other option I could think of was leaving the bank, starting an independent practice that only provided biblically responsible investing services and seeing what happened. But that was nuts, because I didn't have any experience, network, clients, money, or any of the other "requirements" that everyone knows you need to do something like that.

Of course, God has His own way of doing things and much to my amazement as my wife and I prayed, He made it abundantly clear that was the direction He was calling me to go.

I was terrified.

Stepping Out Of The Boat

A couple months of fear and trembling later, I made the decision and stepped out of the bank, out of the proverbial boat, and into an adventure of faith like none I have ever been on before or since.

In April, 2011, I opened the doors to an office that I named Christian Wealth Management with just me and a laptop, no idea what I was doing, less than two months of savings in the bank and fully prepared never to pay my mortgage ever again in my life. I knew that God had called me to this, but I had no idea if it was going to be financially successful or not.

I was keenly aware that the Bible is full of examples of obedient disciples who were rewarded with such earthly experiences like being beheaded, and I had come to the point where I was ready to follow my Lord no matter what the consequence. Preferably not beheading, but that was up to God!

Crazy Love, Crazy Faith

I had just recently read Francis Chan's life-changing book "Crazy Love", which devotes significant page space discussing what it means to really live by faith. Chan observes that we in America tend to think we are "living by faith", but in reality if things don't work out according to plan, we have a safety net: a savings account, job prospects, or some other means to avert complete and utter disaster.

Contrast that with the heroes of faith in the Bible. Abraham had no safety net. Gideon had no safety net. Noah had no safety net. If God did not show up in miraculous fashion, these men (and we'll throw Isaac into that lot, too!) were up the creek without a paddle. Except the creek was full of piranhas, the boat full of holes, and they were taking heavy sniper fire from the shore.

I kind of felt like that, too.

In fact, looking back I believe that was the first time I had ever really been in the position where if God did not supernaturally intervene, I was out of options and things would not be going well for me.

Thankfully, God did show up, and fast.

God Showed Up

Having no idea what else to do, I simply started out educating people about what I had found and what I was doing with biblically responsible investing.

And you know what? Immediately people had the same reaction I did when I first heard about BRI and began asking me questions.

"Wow, I never thought about that before. How do I find out what is in my portfolio?"

"Is it possible to invest any other way?"

"What does a biblically responsible portfolio look like?"

And my little one-man business started growing. Booming, in fact, to the point that I needed to find another advisor to bring into the practice to help with the load of investors God was sending my direction, which was never part of my plan.

My "grand vision" when I started out was, if I was really successful, then I might have an assistant one day a few years down the road. God had other, bigger, plans.

Chapter 2

Inspired

The next thing I know, I am getting phone calls from people all over the country.

This was not expected, as my only non-local marketing channel was something vaguely resembling a website, which I built myself with a free online template and amounted to an online business card: The kind of business card that you have carried around in your pocket for too long until the corners are bent, colors are faded and there is something resembling a tiny piece of melted gummy bear stuck to the front, covered in pocket lint. You get the picture. I was surprised I was getting calls.

Mostly I was getting calls from other financial advisors who were saying that they heard about me and what I was doing with biblically responsible investing and that they were feeling the same tug from the Holy Spirit to make a similar pivot in their career to a BRI practice.

These people were well meaning, but obviously they had lost their mind. I explained to them that I had no idea what I was doing, but they just would not listen to reason. So they, too, left their good paying jobs or turned their existing practices upside down to join this crazy BRI revolution.

One advisor turned into two, which turned into four, which turned into twelve, then twenty, until I had mentored hundreds of Christian financial advisors from all over the country on what we had learned and developed as best practices for successfully running a high quality, biblically responsible investing firm.
God was moving.

And we are still training scores of Christian financial advisors through the Christian Wealth Management network to this day.

Looking For An Answer

Throughout our conversations with advisors, we consistently received one question, "I've built my practice on low cost, index based investment portfolios. Where can I find an index based, biblically responsible solution to use with my clients?"

The answer: "Nowhere."

The only investment funds available back then were

relatively expensive, actively managed mutual funds, with a hit and miss track record of performance. Meanwhile, the mainstream investment industry was making huge shifts toward low cost index funds, and there was no biblically responsible option.

As we went searching for a solution to this problem, some very large secular mutual fund firms expressed interest in creating product for our quickly growing network of advisors and their biblically responsible investor clients. But when we got into the details of what we would screen out of the portfolio – abortion, adult entertainment, LGBT activism and the like – the phones went silent. These secular firms simply couldn't stomach the potential political fallout from managing products that aligned with biblical values.

So one day as our leadership team sat around the boardroom table, we just stared blankly at each other and said, "Well, I guess this means us." And we embarked down the path to create something totally new to bring the biblically responsible investing movement up to speed with the rest of the investing world.

Inspiring Impact

Shortly thereafter, Inspire Investing was born in August of 2015 with zero assets under management (AUM), offering a lineup of index based portfolios that followed diligent, biblically responsible investing principles using what we called the Inspire Impact Score methodology.

We didn't just want to create another screened investment offering that simply "kicked out the bad guys" and invested in what was left over. We wanted an objective, rules based, repeatable methodology to identify the most inspiring, biblically aligned companies in the world to invest in.

We wanted to invest in companies doing amazing things, like working on cures for cancer, creating solutions to provide clean water to people in need, operating with integrity throughout their supply chains, blessing their workforce and their communities: In short, companies that were making the world a better place and "loving their neighbors" well.

We believed these inspiring companies not only represented an opportunity for investors to glorify God with their investment portfolio, but also might provide potential for superior performance based on our preliminary quantitative research, as well as our qualitative perspective on the competitive advantage these businesses of blessing could hold in the marketplace as a result of their ethical practices.

Little did we know our Inspire Impact Score would soon be lauded as a revolutionary advancement in the Environmental/Social/Governance (ESG) investment category, and Inspire products would soon change the global investment landscape.

Inspiring Growth

By the end of 2015, just four months after launch,

Inspire was managing about $25M in AUM. By the end of the following year, Inspire AUM had grown 113% to over $53M and we were recognized for the first time in Financial Advisor Magazine's annual listing of the fastest growing registered investment advisory (RIA) firms in the nation. We didn't even know we made the list until a reporter from the magazine called and asked me for a comment.

When she asked why we were growing so fast and experiencing such success, I told her it was because of God's grace on our lives, that the biblically responsible investing movement was something important to Him, that He wanted his people to manage his money according to his values and that He was moving in a powerful way in the financial industry, inspiring transformation in the hearts and minds of people everywhere. Not the answer she was expecting, I think.

While my quote did not make the print for some reason, the article did mention us and pointed out that Inspire was dedicated to the rapidly growing practice of biblically responsible investing.

New York, New York

On February 28th, 2017, we launched a couple products on the New York Stock Exchange so that more investors could access our biblically responsible, Inspire Impact Score based index strategies through their current brokerage accounts all over the world.

The next day, March 1st, 2017, I received a phone call from a colleague on the east coast asking if I had read The New York Times that morning. Inspire Investing had literally made front-page business news. The headline? "Funds Invoke Bible Values, Others See Intolerance" – right next to an article about newly elected Donald Trump on page B1, above the fold.

While that was not exactly the headline I would have chosen myself, it was still pretty cool. I went to the coffee shop and bought all six copies of The New York Times they had on the shelf.

Global Spotlight On Biblically Responsible Investing

The following days, weeks and months saw a flurry of headlines published about Inspire Investing and our biblically responsible, Inspire Impact Score based index offerings.

Hundreds of articles and TV interviews from the likes of Bloomberg, FOX News, The Wall Street Journal, The Financial Times, Financial Advisor Magazine, ETF Trends, Wealth Management Magazine, Barron's and others spread Inspire's biblically responsible investing message around the world.

Some of this press was enthusiastic about Inspire's mission and the growing numbers of investors aligning their portfolios with biblical values. However, most of the press was antagonistic to our cause of supporting biblical values, and hurled cliché labels, insults and mockery in our direction.

When reporters would call me for interviews, they would always ask – the same incredulous tone of disbelief in their voice – how we expected to be successful advocating for such outdated values that "no one believed in anymore". I was told that we were on the "wrong side of history". I was even asked if I believed that President Donald Trump was God's plan to fix America. I'm not sure what that last question had to do with our investment methodology, but whatever.

Regardless of the positive or negative spin reporters put on our story, as a result of the press investors all over the world were discovering biblically responsible investing for the very first time. Emails, phone calls and even Twitter messages started pouring in from investors in far-flung countries like Zambia, Brazil and Ireland. Also South Korea, but those were harder to read.

And investors here in the United States were also discovering biblically responsible investing in droves, and in some cases re-discovering BRI but getting involved for the first time. The biblically responsible investing movement was catching fire and gathering momentum like I had never seen before.

We got a lot of praise for our masterfully executed PR strategy. The only thing was, we didn't have a PR strategy. All of that press came out of nowhere.
Only God could have done such a thing.

Inspiring Transformation

It was remarkable to watch the biblically responsible investing movement expand by leaps and bounds.

Ringing the closing bell of the New York Stock Exchange was incredible.

Preaching a sermon at the New York Stock Exchange before ringing the bell and singing "Amazing Grace" on the trading floor during the bell ringing was even more incredible.

It was an honor to be named as a finalist for both the 2017 "Best New ESG ETF" and "Best ETF Issuer" of the year award from ETF.com.

It was exhilarating opening up the annual FA Magazine "Top 50 Fastest Growing Firms" report and seeing Inspire ranked #5 in the nation for 2017.

But what has been even more remarkable is watching God use this scrappy little firm out in California and the collective voice of Christian investors around the world to inspire transformation for His glory.
By the grace of God, we have seen some of the largest companies in the world change their policies about where they donate corporate funds, ending their corporate support of Planned Parenthood and other immoral organizations – all because of our corporate engagement efforts.

And through our Inspire Give50 program, where we donate 50% or more of our corporate profits to Christian ministry each year, we are also blessed by God to have been able to drill a clean water well for an impoverished village in Nepal, send Bibles covertly into North Korea, share the hope of the Gospel with thousands of youth in America, provide pro-life counseling to abortion vulnerable mothers, and adopt an entire village high in the coffee farming mountains of Guatemala to build a church, provide clean water, supply a medical clinic, improve education and sponsor children to completely transform the lives of those who live there in the name of Jesus Christ.

Feeble First Step

I really can't believe where God has brought the BRI movement over the past number of years. And I really can't believe where God has brought me over the past number of years. I am a weak and unworthy man. There are countless others who are more intelligent, more driven, more charismatic, better educated, more experienced, better connected and better funded than I. But for some reason, God saw fit to do something with my five loaves and two fish.

I begin this book with my story not because I want everyone to know what I have accomplished, but because I want everyone to know what God has accomplished, and is still accomplishing. "In the same way, let your light shine before others, so that they may see your good works and give glory to your Father who is in heaven." (Matthew 5:16)

And I want everyone to know what God can accomplish through them, through you, if you will listen for His voice, trust Him and step out of the boat.

God is on the move in the world of investing. There is something truly special going on right now, and you have the opportunity to get involved and be part of it. Christians everywhere are changing the way they invest for the glory of God, and corporations are taking notice and listening to the collective voice of Christian investors as we graciously and humbly express our support for biblical values.

But, it all starts with a single step of faith. And it is a step of faith to invest biblically, make no mistake. The world will not understand, and so called experts will scoff. But, all glory to God for what He can do with a feeble first step of faith.

Will you follow His lead, no matter the cost?

Chapter 3

Whatever You Do

At its most basic, biblically responsible investing is the practice of taking 1 Corinthians 10:31 at face value, "So whether you eat or drink or whatever you do, do all to the glory of God." If you and I can eat and drink to the glory of God, surely we can (and should!) invest to the glory of God.

Often, BRI is misunderstood as simply a "financial boycott" that is designed to "stick it to the man" and punish "evil companies", and other terms and concepts that require "quotation marks" around them. And although there is an element of avoiding investments in immoral companies, and sometimes companies can be influenced because of that, the true heart and purpose of BRI is far from that.

It is instead a heart of worship that desires to glorify God in all we do, to shine the light of Christ brightly that the world "may see your good works and give glory to your Father who is in heaven" (Matthew 5:16). Even if companies never changed a thing about the values they support or products and services they sell, biblically responsible investing would still be important because it is ultimately not about changing the world, but about glorifying our Father who is in heaven.

Put another way, BRI is not about the responsibility of companies to act justly and morally, but rather BRI is all about your responsibility to glorify God to the fullest extent possible with everything He has given you.
And hey, if the world changes for the better in the meantime, what a bonus!

Three Strand Cord

Practically speaking, there are three aspects involved in a comprehensive approach to biblically responsible investing.

Endorse

First, biblically responsible investors seek to endorse companies which are acting in alignment with biblical values and more closely express God's heart towards His creation. These companies are a blessing to their customers, their communities, their workforce and the world. They are creating inspiring, beneficial products and services that add value to the lives of their customers. They are operating with high levels of integrity throughout their operations. They are involved in giving back to their communities in which they operate and they provide their employees with outstanding workplace experience.

There are numerous categories and subcategories to examine companies in this way, typically categorized under the Environmental, Social and Governance (ESG) framework, and though the purpose of this book is not to give a detailed account of every ESG issue under the sun, some specific examples include:

- A textile company that goes above and beyond to investigate every nook and cranny of their supply chain to ensure that there are no child labor or sweat shop operations feeding their product lines;
- A pharmaceutical company working on innovative treatments for diseases like cancer, Alzheimer's and Parkinson's;
- A hotel chain that has made the valiant decision to remove pornography from all of their properties, despite the potential loss of revenues;
- A coffee company providing above average benefits and wages to all of their employees;
- An energy company that takes great care in extracting oil to ensure minimal environmental impact and that makes large investments in researching and developing clean energy solutions;
- A hospital operator that protects the rights of the unborn and the well-being of their mothers by refusing to offer abortions in their facilities.

Engage

The second aspect involved in a comprehensive approach to BRI is for investors to engage companies through shareholder activism. This is perhaps one of the most exciting parts of being a biblically responsible investor.

As an owner of a company's stock, you are an owner of that company. And no matter how small a percentage you might own, you are entitled to have your voice heard by the executives and employees at your company.

My friends and I have had the pleasure of engaging with several companies, and by the grace of God we have had some remarkable successes.

Exxon used to give money to an abortion organization that partnered with third-world governments to distribute abortion kits for the purposes of population control. Because of our engagement with them, they stopped.

Chevron was in the practice of making sizeable annual donations to Planned Parenthood, but because of our engagement with them, they stopped.

One of the largest wholesale shopping club chains in the country (who I agreed to keep anonymous to protect the innocent, because no good deed goes unpunished these days) was making donations to several gay pride parades around the country – which are not celebrations of love and equality, but of public lewdness and drunken vulgarity – and because of our engagement, they stopped.

And there are, of course, other companies which did not respond positively to our engagement efforts, but even so with them they are now more aware that there are a group of investors who care about biblical values, who are willing to get involved and make their voice heard, and that will factor into future decision making at those companies and the results are in God's hands.

The simplest form of engaging a company is to find the investor relations page on their website and email or call the investor relations personnel regarding whatever issue you want to discuss. The investor relations people at your company are completely dedicated to communicating with shareholders, encouraging an enthusiastic shareholder community and doing what they can to make people proud to own their stock.

A more involved form of engagement would be to file an actual shareholder resolution with the company, putting forth a measure to be voted on by shareholders at the next annual shareholder meeting, and affording you or your appointed agent the opportunity to stand and speak for a few minutes to the executives and shareholders present at that meeting.

And if all of this sounds rather intimidating for you, the easiest way of all to get involved is to invest with a firm, fund company or advisor who actively engages with companies on your behalf.

Exclude

The third and most widely known aspect of a well-rounded approach to BRI is for an investor to exclude certain companies from their investment portfolio based on selected criterion. To reiterate, the point of exclusion is not to punish companies, but to ensure that your own hands are clean before the Lord.

When you own a company's stock, your returns are derived from the business activities of that company, and that company's activities are reflected on you as an owner. Many investors are shocked to discover the immoral issues that have been festering within their portfolios for years without them knowing about it.

- A "family company" that sells baby shampoo, but also manufactures products specifically for use in abortion procedures;
- A streaming video company that offers a tangled "net" of pornography "flix" among their video titles;
- An online retailer that sells all manner of lewd items online amid the "Amazonian" jungle of other products;
- A retail company with a "targeted" plan to promote an activist LGBT agenda with corporate donations, political lobbying and violating state laws by inviting men into women's changing rooms and restrooms, and vice-versa.

Owner Verses Consumer

At this point, many people ask the question, "If I am excluding these companies from my investment portfolio, does that mean I need to stop shopping with them as well?"

That is a very appropriate question, and the answer is, "Not necessarily".

There is a big difference in responsibility between an owner and a consumer. As an owner, I am responsible for everything my company does. As a consumer, I am only responsible for what I am spending my money on.

I like to use the example of a certain baby shampoo company that we all know and love. My wife and I have four kids and we have bought a lot of baby shampoo from this company over the past 12 years. But, I would never invest in their stock.

Why?

Because in addition to baby shampoo, they also manufacture products that are designed for use in abortion procedures. If I were to own that stock, I would be willingly earning money from the destruction of human life with these products. I cannot tell this company to send me a dividend only from the sale of their baby shampoo and not from the sale of the abortion product. My dividend comes from all of the company's revenue producing activities.

But, as a consumer I am responsible only for what

I purchase. If I were to be a customer of the abortion product, then that is on me. But if I only buy baby shampoo, I have no responsibility whatsoever for the other products that company might be involved with. In fact, my purchases are another way that I can help send a message to this company. By purchasing baby shampoo and not the abortion product, I am telling this company to make more of this and less of that. And I am speaking in the clearest language a business knows: money.

There are times when we as concerned consumers may choose to boycott a company, and I have participated in boycotts myself at times. But the decision to boycott is not a moral imperative. It is a personal decision left up to the individual's conscience. We are free to boycott or not to boycott as the Lord directs our conscience. For a biblical reference, read Paul's instructions to the church in 1 Corinthians 8.

Investing, and I mean ownership, is a completely different ballgame. As an owner I have responsibility. That means that the decision to avoid investments in companies involved in immoral issues is not up to my personal conscience, but rather is a moral directive of biblical stewardship.

Ask yourself this question, which was asked of me when I was first discovering BRI and wrestling through what a God honoring approach looks like:

"How much money is okay to earn from abortion, pornography or other immoral practices?"

The only answer I can come up with is zero. But don't take my word for it. Let's examine what scripture has to say on the issue together.

ROBERT NETZLY

Chapter 4

God's Word On Investing

Did you consult the Bible before you bought into your investment portfolio?

That may seem like a strange question, but the Bible has a lot to say to Christians about how to manage investments, with both financial and moral implications. But many Christians remain unaware of what the Bible teaches on this topic, or worse, they have been taught in a church context something contrary to what God's word says and assume it is from the Bible!

[As a note to any pastors or lay leaders out there, there is a severe lack of biblically sound teaching in our churches today about proper stewardship of investment assets. The most popular stewardship courses cover all the purely practical aspects of investing, like "what is a mutual fund" or "how to diversify", and offer no instruction different than that available from the world outside the church. But none of these courses go into any depth on the spiritual issues related to investing for the glory of God. There are important moral, ethical, and holiness issues that our people need to be taught about investing. If anyone wants to take on that challenge, I would love to help however I can. And now we return to our regularly scheduled programming.]

While scripture provides an immensely deep, bottomless really, pool of wisdom and instruction for Christian investors on both practical matters and matters of practical holiness, we will look at just a few buckets-full from which to drink as I have not the theological skill, nor this book the scope and breadth, to adequately address everything the Bible has to say on the matter of investing.

Here are five Bible verses that every Christian investor should take to heart as they seek to be wise stewards of the money God has placed in their hands.

Investing For The Glory Of God

"So, whether you eat or drink, or whatever you do, do all to the glory of God." (1 Corinthians 10:31)

When you ate your oatmeal this morning, did you realize it was intended to be an act of worship? This verse says plain as day that our purpose for investing, and everything else in life, should be to glorify God.

This may seem like stating the obvious to some, but it is important because this verse is commanding us to intentionally pursue God's glory in every investment decision we make. And God's glory goes far beyond the financial aspect of investing and also includes issues of morality and ethics. To invest for God's glory means that we must consider more than just our financial returns when making an investment.

If we can eat and drink to the glory of God, certainly we can and should invest God's money for God's glory.

Better is a little

"Better is a little with righteousness than great revenues with injustice." (Proverbs 16:8)

This verse could not possibly be more subversively counter-cultural. It flies in the face of all that Wall Street stands for. It contradicts the foundational economic theses of some of the world's foremost financial experts, who boldly proclaim that maximizing profits is the first and only duty of business and investing. (I'm looking at you, Milton Friedman).

And the influence of this worldly perspective on wealth has also infected the Church, resulting in many Christian financial experts regurgitating Wall Street's profit-at-all-cost stump speech. Sometimes these Christian voices even attempt (unsuccessfully) to validate that viewpoint with scripture.

Often they point to the Parable Of The Talents in

Matthew 25 to make the claim that God rewards those most who make the most money. But that parable is not making that claim at all, and even if it was, it does not follow that the Master in that parable does not care about how his servants made his money grow.

What the parable teaches is that God expects us to use everything that He has given us in accordance with His expectations, His values and His will. Newsflash: God doesn't need more money. He certainly could care less about how much money we make "for him" in this life. US Dollars don't spend in Heaven. (Nor do any other dollars or currency, just in case you were wondering.)

Proverbs 16:8 makes it clear that God cares more about how we make money rather than how much money we make. Indeed, God proclaims it is better to produce a lower return on investment in a righteous manner than high-flying profits unjustly. There is nothing wrong with earning high investment returns, but they must never come at the expense of holiness and certainly cannot be our primary directive.

Therefore, it is a biblical imperative that Christian investors consider the moral implications of their investments. Are you earning money from abortion, pornography, human trafficking or other unjust industries? We cannot ignore these issues if we are to be true to God's word.

Indecent Investment Exposure

"Take no part in the unfruitful works of darkness, but

instead expose them." (Ephesians 5:11)

Here is another, more direct command to Christians to not only avoid participation in immorality, but also to expose it for what it really is. We need to call a spade a spade, or in this case, call an immoral investment an immoral investment.

Enlarging your investment account by investing in the "unfruitful works of darkness" is not an option for Christian investors. This is not an issue that the Bible allows us room for personal convictions. It is commanded. Instructed. Required.

Let me also say that there is grace here, too. Some investors are new to this concept of screening their investments based on biblical morality and as such are profiting from activities that would make them shudder. Praise God that He is gracious and willing to forgive our trespasses, including those made in ignorance! Lord knows that I am need of that grace on a daily basis!

Not In My House

"You shall not bring the fee of a prostitute or the wages of a dog into the house of the Lord your God in payment for any vow, for both of these are an abomination to the Lord your God." (Deuteronomy 23:18)

Here we get a strong taste of the Lord's disdain for the wages of immorality. "Abomination" is not a word to be tossed around lightly, and the Bible reserves that word for only the most, well, abominable activities.

It should be well noted by all Christian investors that the Lord does not simply have a passing distaste for the profits from sinful business activity, He abominates them. So much so that God even forbids the money earned from sin to be brought into the house of the Lord and given as an offering. This is no small issue in our Lord's eyes.

I have heard some Christian commentators attempt to make the case that a Christian investor can justify investing in the stock of companies which earn profits from immoral activities as long as the investor donates their portion of the profits generously to ministry, like some sort of spiritual money laundering scheme. Indeed, this same thought passed through my mind some years ago when I first was presented with the unsettling truth that I was invested in and recommending investments in companies with serious moral issues.

This scripture soundly rejects that notion altogether. The ends do not justify the means in God's economy.

Joyful Reward

"His master said to him, 'Well done, good and faithful servant. You have been faithful over a little; I will set you over much. Enter into the joy of your master.'" (Matthew 25:21)

Now back to Matthew 25. For all of the clear instruction to avoid profiting from and participating in works of immorality, there is also a great reward for those who have been faithful in stewarding what God has placed in their hands. And as mentioned earlier, faithfulness to God is not measured in financial currency, but by the measure of God's glory.

There will be great joy for you when you stand before the Lord having faithfully honored Him in your life, by His grace and the Holy Spirit's power. Our labor to honor God is not done from a spirit of fear of punishment, but from a longing to glorify our Lord and receive the "well done" as an eager child from a loving father.

"By this is love perfected with us, so that we may have confidence for the day of judgment, because as he is so also are we in this world. There is no fear in love, but perfect love casts out fear. For fear has to do with punishment, and whoever fears has not been perfected in love. We love because he first loved us." (1 John 4:17-19)

Honor the Lord with all that He has given you. Glorify Him to the utmost in every word, deed and investment. Joyfully submit your portfolio to the lordship of Christ, for it all belongs to Him after all. Eagerly look forward and strive to "enter into the joy of your Master", by the power of the Holy Spirit and the grace of God in your life.

ROBERT NETZLY

Chapter 5

Did God Really Say?

Oldest Trick In The Book

Literally the oldest trick in the book. "Did God really say?" continues to be a favorite tool of the enemy as he "prowls around, like a roaring lion, seeking someone to devour." (1 Peter 5:8)

We first see this snare set in the Garden of Eden, way back in Genesis 3:1, "Now the serpent was more crafty than any other beast of the field that the LORD God had made. He said to the woman, 'Did God really say, 'You shall not eat of any tree in the garden'?"

And you know the rest of the story. How easily we are swayed to doubt God's word!

Whispering Seeds Of Doubt

Adam and Eve walked side by side with God in the cool of the Garden. As yet unstained by sin, they spoke face to face with Him and heard his voice. They stood with Him as He pointed out all the blessings He had created for them, all the trees and plants that were good for food, and the one tree out of all the rest that they were to avoid. Just this one tree. One. Tree.

But along comes the serpent, hissing in their ear seeds of doubt, "Did God really say?" And instantly our first parents choose to believe the lie. To believe the creature instead of the Creator. To doubt the goodness of God's commands, and indeed even to doubt the goodness of God Himself!

And we do the same thing today.

In fact, he may be whispering that to you right now. Having just examined several clear examples from the Bible about the necessity of biblically responsible investing as an integral part of Christian stewardship, it is likely that the enemy would be seeking to cast his seeds of doubt in amongst the truth which was just planted, or if he can, to pluck out the seeds of truth altogether like so many heads of grain upon a rocky path.

Beloved, do not let him.

Old Trick, New Garden

The serpent is still whispering, "Did God really say?", and if we listen to him, "as the serpent deceived Eve by his cunning, your thoughts will be led astray from a sincere and pure devotion to Christ" (2 Corinthians 11:3).

Did God really say that I cannot serve both God and money?

Did God really say He commands me to forgive all who wrong me?

Did God really say not to sin in my anger?

Did God really say to do everything for His glory?

Did God really say all my money is really His money?

Did God really say not to invest in immoral industries like abortion and pornography?

Did God really say that He demands holiness in my relationships, finances, investments, work, thoughts and every other area of life?

Perfect Word

Dear beloved, hear me! The answer is "Yes, God really did say!" Go to His perfect word and soak your sin stained mind in the truth of God! Let it wash over you, cleansing away the serpent filth and reminding you of the truth, goodness and majesty of God! His commands are life and blessing, protection for your soul!

"The law of the LORD is perfect,
reviving the soul;
the testimony of the LORD is sure,
making wise the simple;
the precepts of the LORD are right,
rejoicing the heart;
the commandment of the LORD is pure,
enlightening the eyes;
the fear of the LORD is clean,
enduring forever;
the rules of the LORD are true,
and righteous altogether.
More to be desired are they than gold,
even much fine gold..." (Psalm 19:7-10)

Do you believe this?

Trust in His goodness. Submit to His word. Silence the snake. Love God with all your heart, soul, mind and strength. And investments.

Chapter 6

Saving Babies

Of all the issues that biblically responsible investing addresses, one is particularly close to my heart and, in my opinion, dictates much urgency as there are literally lives at stake. The issue is abortion.

I do not want to downplay the importance of other issues, such as human trafficking or pornography, but when we look at the number of lives lost, and the incredible pain caused to mothers on a scale that is hard to fathom, I believe it valuable to take you into a deep dive on how you can align your investments to support and advance the pro-life movement and help save the lives of countless, precious babies and their mothers who are in danger right now as you read these words.

Growing Pro-Life Movement

Millions upon millions of unborn children have lost their lives to abortion. Thankfully, abortion rates in the US reached the lowest number since Roe v. Wade in recent years and were below one million for the first time since the 70's, according to the latest research by the Guttmacher Institute.

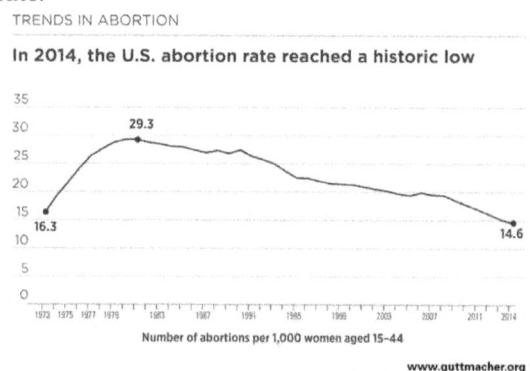

TRENDS IN ABORTION

In 2014, the U.S. abortion rate reached a historic low

Number of abortions per 1,000 women aged 15-44

www.guttmacher.org

There is also growing support for the pro-life movement among younger generations, representing a tide change in public sentiment regarding abortion. Millions of people, young and old, are praying for an end to abortion in our lifetime – and I believe we will see that prayer answered.

As the movement continues to gather steam, more people are diligently making a pro-life impact in an unlikely place: their investment account.

Pro-Life Investing

Many pro-life investors are shocked to discover that they have been profiting from and supporting abortions in their 401(k), IRA, mutual funds and other investment accounts.

But with a little effort it is possible to not only eliminate abortion from your portfolio, but to actually support the pro-life movement with your investment decisions.

So, how does the abortion industry get into your investment portfolio? Here are five abortion issues that are commonly found in mutual funds and other investments:

- **Abortion drugs:** This one is obvious, but remarkably overlooked by pro-life investors. The pharmaceutical companies that manufacture and distribute abortifacient drugs are commonly included in many of the most popular mutual funds, and as such many pro-life advocates are unwittingly profiting from the sale of abortion drugs.

- **Abortion facilities:** Many hospitals and clinics which provide abortion procedures are owned by publicly traded companies, and in some cases the hospital or other organization is a publicly traded company itself. As such, these stocks routinely make their way into the investment portfolios of investors around the country.

- **Legislation and promotion:** Some companies which are not directly involved in abortions from a business standpoint choose to throw around their corporate clout in support of abortion through fighting for anti-life abortion legislation or providing marketing campaigns and other promotional support for abortion.

- **Philanthropy:** Many companies give charitable contributions to Planned Parenthood and other abortion organizations that pro-life investors would never dream of giving a penny to.

- **Biotech:** Issues such as fetal stem cell research and cloning, or even using the discarded body parts of aborted babies, are widespread in the biotech industry. Pro-life investors should endeavor to avoid companies that choose to wade in those polluted waters, and when making an investment in the biotech sector should take great care that their companies are not entangled in the abortion mafia.

Under the surface

If you want to find out if any of these abortion issues are lurking in your investment portfolio, there are tools available to help you. Many Christian financial advisors, such as those who are members of Christian Wealth Management, have access to software that drills down into your stocks, bonds, mutual funds, ETFs and other investments and analyzes the granular data of what the companies you own are involved in from a pro-life perspective.

And if you are more of a do-it-yourselfer, you can easily screen your investments yourself for free at www.inspireinsight.com by just typing in your ticker symbols. The results are often eye-opening.

As I mentioned in my own BRI discovery story, this issue in particular was what opened my eyes to the need for a change in my own investments. There I sat on the board of our local pro-life pregnancy center, and yet I owned numerous stock positions in companies that were manufacturing abortion drugs, operating abortion facilities and donating money to Planned Parenthood.

That's what I call convicting. And that discovery changed my life forever.

I am warning you, if you want to be blissfully unaware and just continue investing with your eyes closed, do not search this information out because once you know you can never go back.

But if you do decide to peel back the veneer and see what is underneath the polished exterior of Wall Street's investment offerings, this data will arm you with the information you need to take steps to eliminate abortion from your portfolio and start supporting the pro-life movement with your investments.

Saving babies

When you invest biblically responsibly, whether on your own, through a fund company or through your financial advisor, your money is not only working toward your financial goals but also helping to support the pro-life movement. Together, we as Christians are sending a powerful message to the boardrooms of corporations across the country and around the world that the lives of the unborn matter and we will not stand to share in the profits of the shedding of innocent blood.

The BRI community also engages with corporations on a regular basis to advocate for biblical values. By God's grace we have several pro-life investing success stories of major corporations ending donations to Planned Parenthood and other abortion organizations. And by God's grace we will have many, many more of those stories as pro-life investors put their money where their values are. The more assets we manage biblically responsibly, the more influence we have with companies to inspire transformation. When you invest biblically responsibly, you are adding your voice to those of pro-life investors around the world and together we are making a difference!

In just a handful of years, we could see abortion wiped out in America. And you can help right now by aligning your investments to save the babies.

Will you join us?

Chapter 7

Christian Loser Weirdo

I've been called a lot of names in my life, but Christian-loser-weirdo has got to take the cake.

This notable appellation was donned upon me by a financial advisor from the east coast who had come across a webinar invitation for Inspire Investing. His email reply was not exactly typical, but not surprising to us anymore as we get some rather interesting communiqué from time to time, as you might imagine a company like ours does that advocates for biblical values on Wall Street.

His email read (all formatting, including ALL CAPS, are true to the original email):

> "RELIGION IS THE BIGGEST PONZI SCHEME MAN EVER CREATED!!!!!!!!!!!!!!!!!!!!!!!

> !!!!!! DO NOT SEND ME THIS CRAP EVER AGAIN!!!!!!!!!!!!!!!!!!!!!!!!! !!!!!!!!!!!!!!! !!!!!!!!!!! SHAME ON YOU, LOSER!!!!!!!!!! !!"

[and a second email a few seconds later…]

> "AND, NO, I'M NOT AFRAID OF BURNING IN HELL YOU WIERDO !!!!!!!!!!!!!!!!!!!!!!!!! !!!!!!!!!!!!!!!!!!!!!!!!!"

I'm not sure why he brought up burning in hell, because we certainly didn't. There is obviously more going on there than we know.

My point in sharing this is, that as we set out to honor God with our investment decisions, we must also remember another passage of scripture that I have found very applicable, "Blessed are you when others revile you and persecute you and utter all kinds of evil against you falsely on my account. Rejoice and be glad, for your reward is great in heaven, for so they persecuted the prophets who were before you" (Matthew 5:11-12).

And another that is like it, "If you are insulted for the name of Christ, you are blessed, because the Spirit of glory and of God rests upon you" (1 Peter 4:14).

If you make the decision to follow Christ down the path of biblically responsible investing, you will meet resistance. Certainly, there are likeminded brothers and sisters who will joyfully link arms with you down the straight and narrow, but there will also be those who mock you. There will be those who roll their eyes at you as they would a day-dreaming child. And there may even be those who outright oppose you with such venomous audacity that your heart skips a beat.

At least, that has been my experience.

Maybe this resistance comes from a relative as you talk about the stock market over dinner. Maybe it comes from your boss when you ask about adding biblically responsible investing options in your 401(k). Or maybe it even comes from your spouse as you discuss how to invest for your retirement. Jesus promised us trials in this world if we would follow after him, "In this world you will have tribulation" (John 16:33), and that promise rings true in the area of finances as it does in other areas of life.

Granted, given my media exposure I tend to be a much more visible target than the average investor, and it is unlikely that you will start receiving emails from random people around the globe like I do. But, I want to share with you just a few more email messages I have received in response to my involvement in the biblically responsible investing movement to give you a concrete example of the spiritual opposition that awaits all who follow Christ.

Some of the emails I have received are not fit to print in a civilized publication for civilized readers, and others are not fit to even be mentioned. But among those that are less vulgar or otherwise inappropriate, below are some choice examples. As you read these, remember that, "we do not wrestle against flesh and blood, but against the rulers, against the authorities, against the cosmic powers over this present darkness, against the spiritual forces of evil in the heavenly places" (Ephesians 6:12). There is indeed a spiritual battle being waged every moment of every day, and there is a spiritual battle being waged over your heart and your treasure, for "Where your treasure is, there your heart will be also" (Matthew 6:21).

This was a response to a press release we sent out about a new biblically responsible index:

> "I am so sick of narrow minded bigots...Leave me out of your hate."

And here is a message that someone sent through the contact form on our website:

> "DO NOT EVER send me [marketing information] from your organization again! I am a GAY MAN who has an awesome relationship with God. I was born into a great Christian Family with loving values and a solid home. Based on your ad your organization is nothing but a masked hate group and a scam and markets hate through investments. I am very successful and contribute my success to the idea that I accept and love everyone for who they are and help them stand on their own feet - not stand over them judging them by their sexuality or if they watch porn or not. I am the Co-founder and Chief Operating Officer of a large private Wealth Management team. We invest our clients' $$ based

on asset allocation and risk NOT so called "Biblical Values." I will never invest in your product and will tell all of my friends and colleagues in the investment community to never invest in your product either. I have donated my own time with sweat and tears to less fortunate families (and homeless LGBT youth) and given millions of my own $$ to help people in need and teach them loving values – NOT "Invest like a Christian." -Happy Holidays!"

Other messages have been heavy with explicatives, told us to burn in hell, and some have even threatened physical harm. Why? Because we believe in biblical values as it relates to sexuality, the right to life, justice, decency and holiness. And because we encourage people to invest according to those values.

Sorry if I just made you all depressed. That is not my goal, but sometimes to have meaningful joy, we have to spend some time in the house of somber reflection, "Sorrow is better than laughter, for by sadness of face the heart is made glad" (Ecclesiastes 7:3).

For me, when I read these kind of emails I am reminded that this is yet another proof that it matters what we invest in as Christians. Why would the enemy be so adamantly opposed to something that had no value for godliness in your life? Why would the world mock and deride something unless it was the wisdom and truth of God? These are serious considerations, and powerful evidences for the importance and critical role that biblically responsible investing plays in glorifying God with the money He has entrusted to you for a short while here on earth.

Not alone

But it is also good to remember that we are not alone and that there are many fellow pilgrims with us on the road to glory, all who share our suffering for the name of Christ and our rejoicing in His glory. Here are a few more emails I have received of a very different nature:

This is an email I received from an investor in Africa:

> "Hi Robert,
> I am [their name] and I just started out as an Investor Behavior Consultant. I just wanted to say "you are an inspiration to all Believers around the world!"

And here is a Twitter message I received from another investor in Africa, Zambia to be exact:

> "Hi Robert. I have viewed your website and it seems we have the same passion. God first. Business and investing. May God continue to bless the work you are doing!"

And here is my absolute favorite, an email from an investor in Canada who had his entire outlook on investing changed for the glory of God,

> "Hello,
> I just wanted to send a quick note to let you know that your [blog content] has completely changed the

way I think about my investments. My wife and I do not have a big portfolio and had planned to simply invest our retirement savings in a few good mutual funds.

I had never really thought about what I was profiting from, until I came across Socially Responsible Investing funds - which eventually led me to [biblically responsible investing funds]. I felt a real conviction that I cannot be good a steward of the finances God has given me if I am making money from things that break His heart.

As a Canadian, I do not have access to Christian mutual funds, so I decided to learn how to trade ETFs and opened an account with a brokerage just so that I could invest directly in [biblically responsible] funds. This shift in investment strategy has pushed me to learn everything I can about self-directed investing, and now feel like I am truly in control of where I invest our family's money.

It is so easy as a North American Christian to allow our ignorance to be bliss. We invest in things we morally oppose, but can turn a blind eye to it because we are one step removed from actually purchasing shares in objectionable companies or industries. While it takes a little more work to find and invest directly in companies that are doing good, I am so glad that I took this step because now I know that I am truly honouring God with all my money and I am not trading what is right for what is profitable.

> I would never have stepped out in faith to try self-directed investing if it wasn't for [your blog] posing uncomfortable questions for me to ask myself...
>
> Thank you for your work, and I hope you continue to have great success!"

Life giving

Messages like these are so life-giving to me. It is easy to get myopically focused on the negative notes and the hateful voices of opposition (as they are typically the loudest). But these sweet letters of love and encouragement remind me that God is sovereign, that He has his people all over the world and that I am not alone.

Immediately after talking about wrestling against the spiritual forces of evil in Ephesians chapter 6 which we discussed earlier, the apostle Paul continues on to say,
"Therefore, take up the whole armor of God, that you may be able to withstand in the evil day, and having done all, to stand firm. Stand therefore, having fastened on the belt of truth, and having put on the breastplate of righteousness, and, as shoes for your feet, having put on the readiness given by the gospel of peace. In all circumstances take up the shield of faith, with which you can extinguish all the flaming darts of the evil one; and take the helmet of salvation, and the sword of the Spirit, which is the word of God, praying at all times in the Spirit, with all prayer and supplication" (Ephesians 6:13-18).

May God grant you the grace to put on the full armor

that only He can provide, enabling you to stand firm in the battle that He has already won, but that we are still fighting, until that glorious day when the fight is over and we enter our Master's rest!

Good Christians are fools

As a Christian, wisdom requires you to be a fool – in life, business, family, investing, and every area. You will be called on by Wisdom to make decisions that seem folly to bystanders. Onlookers will mock you at best and do their best to destroy you at worst. They will not understand, accept or even tolerate your path, but you will be anchored by the irrefutable conviction that your decision is right. Because beyond the current affairs of the day, the opinions of the age, and even the temporal success of your endeavors, above all is the timeless and eternal wisdom of God revealed in the Bible. "We have this as a sure and steadfast anchor of the soul..." (Hebrews 6:19).

I can only speak from my own experiences, and I boast in nothing save Jesus Christ alone who is my only glory and sure foundation. Such experiences as when I was compelled to leave the safety and security of my position at the big bank, being compelled by the Spirit to start a company dedicated to biblically responsible investing, with no income, no savings and no clue what I was doing. People questioned my judgement and whispered about the likelihood of my failure.

And when I steadfastly built that business by God's grace, offering only biblically responsible investments, ready to refuse potential revenue under the conviction of scripture that "whatever you do, whether you eat or drink or whatever you do, do all to the glory of God" (1 Corinthians 10:31), many chided my foolishness that I would fail with such a narrow-minded focus, and yet God brought me more investors than I could handle, and also brought me advisor partners who shared my conviction to expand the scale of our growing firm.

Industry experts warned, and even scolded, that my insistence on diligent, biblical screening which filtered out hot-button issues such as LGBT activism and corporate giving to Planned Parenthood was just too radical, unnecessary and intolerant. But how could I in good conscience profit from and recommend such things when scripture's clarion call to "take no part in the unfruitful deeds of darkness, but instead expose them" (Ephesians 5:11) resonated so in my soul?

And when God laid on my heart the necessity to bring biblically responsible investing to the world by launching Inspire, the world was incredulous – and even a bit outraged as we have seen from the emails I shared with you – that we would manage investments aligned with conservative, biblical values instead of conforming to "the pattern of the world".

The media skewered us for our "intolerance"[1]. Financial experts scoffed "thou shalt not buy biblically responsible [investments]"[2] claiming we would never be able to

---

[1] (Moyer 2017)
[2] (Ritholtz 2017)

achieve good performance because of our "limited" investment universe of companies aligned with biblical values. Liberal activists proclaimed that we would never attract investor capital because our "approach is squarely at odds with that of nearly all of corporate America"[3].

And these same pundits scratched their heads when Inspire attracted massive capital, grew assets by 131% and was named among the nation's fastest growing investment firms in the nation, with all glory to God because by worldly standards these authorities should have been right, save for one glaring omission in their reasoning which makes all the difference: God is sovereign. And even if God had seen fit to allow me to fail in the world's economy, I would still be a success in God's economy, which is the only market that really matters after all.

So, when you are faced with a mocking crowd and find your convictions at odds with popular opinion, stand firm in the wisdom of God expressed in the Holy Bible. Stand upon the firm foundation, which is Jesus Christ our Lord, "for the wisdom of this world is folly with God"
(1 Corinthians 3:19).

"Blessed is the man
    who walks not in the counsel of the wicked,
nor stands in the way of sinners,
    nor sits in the seat of scoffers;
but his delight is in the law of the Lord,
    and on his law he meditates day and night.

---

[3] (Moyer 2017)

He is like a tree
>   planted by streams of water
> that yields its fruit in its season,
>   and its leaf does not wither.
> In all that he does, he prospers.
> The wicked are not so,
>   but are like chaff that the wind drives away.
>
> Therefore the wicked will not stand in the judgment,
>   nor sinners in the congregation of the righteous;
> for the Lord knows the way of the righteous,
>   but the way of the wicked will perish" (Psalm 1).

With that truth firmly in our spirit, let us consider some of the temptations the enemy has set to derail our best God glorifying intentions, because if you see the hook it is easier not to take the bait.

Chapter 8

Does Your Conscience Have A Price?

You probably remember the 1993 movie "Indecent Proposal" even if you never saw it (which I hope is the case…bleh) because of it's infamous plot line: a billionaire offers a young couple $1,000,000 for one night with the wife. Indecent proposal indeed.

The plot is brilliant, even if the movie is not, because it touches a very human issue that we all are confronted with on a daily basis: Does your conscience have a price? In our modern day of finance, where Wall Street calls for high profits and low fees above all else, the Christian investor must seriously consider whether there is a return high enough, or fee low enough, that would entice them to abandon God's call to biblically responsible investing.

Make good choices

Every day, moment by moment, we are forced to choose between upholding good ethics and morals, or giving in to the temptations of our baser desires. Sometimes the decision to do the right thing may come almost effortlessly, like opening a door for an old woman, or choosing to pay for your candy bar instead of stealing it away in your pocket. But it wasn't always that way, was it? There was a time in all our lives (hopefully when we were very young!) when the temptation of the forbidden candy bar held an irresistible allure and we really had to wrestle with ourselves to ensure that candy bar did not end up sneaking out of the store in our larcenous little pocket.

When we were a child, the price of our conscience may have been scant more than a candy bar. But now, as adults, does our conscience still have a price, albeit a much higher one? Put another way, is there some payoff high enough that would cause you to accept an "indecent proposal"?

In our best moments, and only by the grace of God, our answer is no. There is no payment high enough, nor penalty great enough, that would cause me to sin against my God. But in our worst moments, the answer unfortunately is yes. And often the price is ridiculously low. The Apostle Paul embodies this struggle as he was led by the Holy Spirit to write,

"For I know that nothing good dwells in me, that is, in my flesh. For I have the desire to do what is right, but not the ability to carry it out. For I do not do the good I want, but the evil I do not want is what I keep on doing... Wretched man that I am! Who will deliver me from this body of death? Thanks be to God through Jesus Christ our Lord!" (Romans 7:18-19,24-25).

50 shades of neon

Today, the siren's call to Christian investors is to join the world and chase high returns and lower fees no matter what. On one hand you have unscrupulous brokers promising sky-high returns with investments in the booming marijuana business, cryptocurrencies (aka. Bitcoin, et al), gold, silver and ocean front property in Arizona. These con jobs are usually pretty easy to spot, especially because the popup ads they use are about 50 different colors of neon and size 3,000 extra-super-bold font. As silly and ridiculous as these gigs are, there are many who fall prey to their allure of greed. I know because some have come seeking my advice after losing their shirts.

But what about other businesses, such as abortion and pornography? If you asked the average Christian investor if they would consider buying into the porn business, they would probably (hopefully!) say no. But, if you asked the average Christian investor if they would consider buying into the porn business for a 100% annual return on their money...well...

I submit to you that this scenario is playing out every single day with Christian investors around the world, except instead of 100% annual returns, Christians are selling out for much, much less. In fact, in some cases they are selling out for less than the price of a candy bar.

Allow me to explain.

King Solomon talks biblically responsible investing

Let's say you have $50,000 to invest. Where will you put it? Many investors, including Christian investors, will end up buying a mutual fund or ETF (exchange traded fund) of some sort. Maybe you would choose the highest performing actively managed fund you can find, or maybe you would focus on investing in the lowest cost index fund available. In either case, you would sensibly be trying to maximize your return (either through stellar investment management or by saving money on fees), but is that a biblical approach?

There is nothing wrong with investing in high performing funds, and certainly there is no problem with keeping fees low with index investing (I happen to be a fan), but for the Christian investor there are other — and I dare say more important — issues to consider, namely those of biblical morals.

Hear again the words of Solomon, "Better is a little with righteousness than great revenues with injustice" (Proverbs 16:8). In this verse and others like it, the Bible's clear teaching is that righteousness is more important than financial gain. Biblically responsible investing (BRI) is the practice of making biblical values the first priority in investment decisions as an obedient act of worship for the glory of God.

This means aligning your investments with biblical values, avoiding companies involved in immoral businesses like abortion and pornography, and instead choosing investments in companies which are a blessing to their customers, communities, workforce and the world — and then taking into consideration maximizing returns and minimizing expenses within the context of the available, biblically responsible investment options.

The problem is that, by and large, Christian investors have gotten this process backward. They heed the advice of Wall Street first and God second. (That is never a good idea, by the way.) They put first priority on finding the highest performing, lowest cost investments without giving thought to the moral concerns of those investments. Or if they do consider biblical values it is only as an afterthought and results in a portfolio that might employ a few screens, such as tobacco or alcohol, but falls far short of the standard of diligently stewarding God's assets in accordance with his values for His glory.

We have caved into the demand of this age that we fulfill our "fiduciary duty" to keep fees as low as possible and returns as high as possible, and abandoned our first and eternally more important "stewardship duty" to "honor God with your wealth" (Proverbs 3:9). We have been "conformed to the pattern of this world" (Romans 12:2) and are bowing down to the idols of low fees and high returns.

And, by the way, just because you put biblical values first does not mean that you must sacrifice returns. Research by Wharton School of Business[4], Oxford University[5], Biola University[6] and many other leading institutions all have concluded that employing values based screening like biblically responsible investing does not negatively affect performance. In fact, some report findings that screening actually can help improve performance.

Some critics say biblically responsible investing advocates use the Bible as an excuse for charging higher fees or being lazy about choosing quality investments. I disagree. I think those critics use low fees and the ever-elusive seduction of higher returns as an excuse for their financial idolatry.

Now what about that candy bar?

To make matters worse, the price we have accepted in this compromise of financial idolatry is often pathetically small. Going back to that $50,000 investment you have to make, let's say that you chose to invest in a very low cost fund that had a total expense ratio of 0.10%. And let's say that there was an equivalent, biblically responsible investing fund with an expense ratio of 1.00%. That means that you chose to prioritize lower fees above biblical values for a total savings of 0.90% per year. Putting that into dollars, that means that you decided to invest in abortion, pornography, human trafficking and other immoral industries instead of honoring God first

---

[4] (Wharton School of Business: University of Pennsylvania 2015)
[5] (Oxford University and Arabesque Partners 2015)
[6] (Enete 2018)

for a total annual savings of $450/year ($50,000 x 0.009 = $450). That is just $1.23 per day…the price of a cheap candy bar.

But, you might say, what if I have much more than $50,000 to invest? My savings would be higher than just a candy bar! Yes, this is true. If you have more than $50,000 to invest then your nominal savings goes up some, so maybe your price to sell out on God is a latte per day instead of a candy bar. Or maybe you have millions of dollars to invest and your savings would be measured in thousands of dollars. Maybe you have so much money that your savings would be, oh, let's say an even $1,000,000. Is that a high enough price for you to accept the "indecent proposal" of Wall Street billionaires?

Wall Street would applaud your "wisdom" as a "good fiduciary". The Bible would call that idolatry.

Grace, truth and biblically responsible investing

Now, let me be the first to confess that I invested as an idolater for years, never realizing that I was investing in and profiting from the vilest sin and immorality the depraved human mind can conjure. And I want you to know that I have a lot of grace for those still investing the way of the world, because I know that most Christian investors are just like I was, unwittingly investing in atrocities because they have never been taught to think biblically about their investments. And this is exactly what needs to change.

We need to heed the call in Romans 12:2, "Do not be

conformed to this world, but be transformed by the renewal of your mind, that by testing you may discern what is the will of God, what is good and acceptable and perfect." We need to extend grace to our brothers and sisters who are caught up in the world's ways, and at the same time we need to understand that ignorance is not an excuse.

In the words of the Apostle Paul, we need to:

"…equip the saints for the work of ministry, for building up the body of Christ, until we all attain to the unity of the faith and of the knowledge of the Son of God, to mature manhood, to the measure of the stature of the fullness of Christ, so that we may no longer be children, tossed to and fro by the waves and carried about by every wind of doctrine, by human cunning, by craftiness in deceitful schemes. Rather, speaking the truth in love, we are to grow up in every way into him who is the head, into Christ, from whom the whole body, joined and held together by every joint with which it is equipped, when each part is working properly, makes the body grow so that it builds itself up in love" (Ephesians 4:12-16).

And it starts with you. It starts with looking in the mirror of God's perfect word, submitting to the call to "do all to the glory of God" (1 Corinthians 10:31), including managing your investments, and then making the change to become a biblically responsible investor who puts righteousness and biblical morals in higher preference than fees and performance.

It continues by you doing your part to "equip the saints for the work of ministry" and sharing what you have learned about the importance of being obedient to God with your investment decisions with the other Christians in your life. Will you join us?

Beloved Christian, Wall Street is beckoning you to invest in immoral industries with the ephemeral allure of higher profits and lower fees. What is your answer to Wall Street's "indecent proposal"?

ROBERT NETZLY

Chapter 9

Dear Rich People

If you are holding this book, you are most likely rich.

You may not feel like you are rich, but you are. You live in a house. You probably drive a car. You have some money. You eat food every day. You have clothes on your back and in your closet. If you get hurt, you can get medical care. If you have young children, they can go to school. The water you drink does not make you sick with parasites.

And not only that, but you also have such luxuries as a TV, smart phone, computer, furniture, dishes and cookware, household decorations, jewelry, a refrigerator, a stove, oven and microwave.

Most people around the world do not have these things. You, my friend, are rich.

Shiny objects

And yet, if you are like me, too often you are not content with what you have. You forget how much you are truly blessed and your naturally covetous heart hungers for more. You flip through fashion catalogs and browse real estate websites or ogle the shiny objects in television commercials, not realizing you are traipsing dangerously around a favorite snare of the enemy: the desire to be rich.

Hear me clearly. I am not condemning you or anyone for being rich, but I am warning you and me both against the danger of the desire to be rich. Can we say along with Paul, "But godliness with contentment is great gain, for we brought nothing into the world, and we can take nothing out of the world. But if we have food and clothing, with these we will be content" (1 Timothy 6:6-8)?

And how does this relate to your motivations for investing? Is your desire to invest successfully really just another expression of your hunger to add to your hoard?

How easy it is to desire to be rich. We certainly do not desire to be poor, do we? But in the scriptures Paul issues a sobering warning to Timothy that those who desire to be rich run afoul with all sorts of disaster. "But those who desire to be rich fall in to temptation, into a snare, into many senseless and harmful desires that plunge people into ruin and destruction. For the love of money is a root of all kinds of evils. It is through this craving that some have wandered away from the faith and pierced themselves with many pangs" (1 Timothy 6:9-10).

I don't know about you, but this causes me to pause and examine my heart because "ruin and destruction" are certainly not part of my long term financial goals.

But is wanting to be rich really against biblical teaching? Yes, yes it is. Consider that in the very next verse Paul exhorts Timothy (and all Christians, including you and me) saying, "But as for you, O man of God, flee these things" (1 Timothy 6:11). God does not want His children chasing after riches any more than a mother wants her child to chase a ball across a busy street. It is not that the object being chased is necessarily wrong, but that the chase will absolutely end in ruin. Take note that Paul is not warning against riches, but rather the desire to be rich. But isn't the desire to be rich what drives our entire economic and investment system?

Yes, yes it is.

This is a problem because it is quite apparent by even the most cursory survey of the culture around us that most people desire to be rich, which means that they are careening headfirst into "many senseless and harmful desires that plunge people into ruin and destruction". They are chasing their ball across the autobahn and the resulting carnage is all around us: Broken marriages, corrupt businesses, exploitation of the poor, families left destitute by dad's (or mom's) excessive risk taking.

And Christians are just as guilty as everyone else. In fact, many popular "prosperity gospel" preachers actually teach their adherents that they should desire to be rich, and that they should petition God loudly and persistently for material wealth, and that riches are a sign of strong faith. This is pure theological sewage and if someone is trying to feed it to you run away as fast as possible. The prosperity "gospel" is not the gospel at all. It is exactly what Paul describes in our text, a "temptation, a snare" that "plunge people into ruin and destruction". Flee from it.

And even if you and I are not drinking from the sewer water that so many prosperity preachers are serving up, it is still far too easy in our culture to desire to be rich without even realizing it. How many times have I desired a bigger house, nicer car, expensive clothes, bigger income, lavish vacations, high-performing investments? Or in other words, how often do I desire to be rich?

And don't we see the damage even these "normal" American desires can be? We are tempted to buy as much house as we can qualify for, the nicest car we can finance and the largest credit limit we can get approved for. The result is often disastrous. Lost house. Lost car. Mountains of debt. Ruined life. The desire to be rich is insidious.

So, what are we to do? Thankfully Paul does not leave us hanging, but continues, "As for the rich in this present age, charge them not to be haughty, nor to set their hopes on the uncertainty of riches, but on God, who richly provides us with everything to enjoy. They are to do good, to be rich in good works, to be generous and ready to share, thus storing up treasure for themselves as a good foundation for the future, so that they may take hold of that which is truly life" (1 Timothy 6:17-19).

Ruin and destruction? No thanks. Kill the desire to be rich.

Everything to enjoy? Count me in.

No Satisfaction

Besides, riches never satisfy those who love them anyway. So why do we chase after them? It is a vain pursuit. "He who loves money will not be satisfied with money, nor he who loves wealth with his income; this also is vanity" (Ecclesiastes 5:10).

What a tragic irony this is: Those who love money will never be satisfied with it. And what a beautiful irony this is: Those who care nothing for money are satisfied already. Oh, how I want to be in the camp of the satisfied! Don't you?

Jesus Christ is our satisfaction! Look nowhere else! It was not on accident that Jesus taught us, "No one can serve two masters, for either he will hate the one and love the other, or he will be devoted to the one and despise the other. You cannot serve both God and money" (Matthew 6:24).

Consider what Jesus is saying:

If we love money, we will hate God. If we are devoted to money, we will despise God.

But if we love God, we will hate money. If we are devoted to God, we will despise money.

You and I cannot serve both God and money. Those two paths are diametrically opposed. Some may try to follow both, to keep one foot upon each path. They want to pursue the treasures of this world and still be promised treasure in heaven. But Jesus says it is either both feet on the straight and narrow way that leads to life, or nothing. It is all for Christ, else it is chasing after the wind down the broad and wide that leads to destruction. "Do not lay up for yourselves treasures on earth, where moth and rust destroy and where thieves break in and steal, but lay up for yourselves treasures in heaven, where neither moth nor rust destroys and where thieves do not break in and steal. For where your treasure is, there your heart will be also" (Matthew 6:19-21).

I used to understand this verse in the wrong way. When I heard "where your treasure is, there your heart will be also", what I thought Jesus was saying is that we put our treasure into things that we care about, that are close to our heart. But one day I realized that is completely backwards.

When Jesus says, "where your treasure is, there your heart will be also", he is saying that our heart follows our treasure! Stop and consider the implications of this for a moment. Our hearts follow our treasure.

Where is your treasure? Figuratively speaking, where are the things that are most valuable to you? Is it your favorite sports team? Is it your job? Is it your social status? Your education? Your family?

These are the potential idols in your life, because as Jesus said, "there your heart will be also". We are drawn to care about those things we treasure. And when we treasure something apart from Christ, if our treasuring of that thing does not flow into worship of God for providing it for us, then we end up worshiping the creation instead of the Creator (Romans 1:25). That is the definition of idolatry, and all of us are only half a step away from the idol factory on any given day.

So, that is figuratively speaking, but what about literally speaking? Where is your literal treasure? Is your treasure invested in companies that advocate for abortion, advance LGBT activism or profit from pornography? If so, your heart will be drawn toward those companies and there is competition for your devotion to God and God's moral law.

Don't believe me? I have seen it over and over again, such as with this investor that we will call "Sally".

Sally's story

Sally heard about me and my biblically responsible investing work and reached out one day to set an appointment to talk. When she came into the office, I helped her discover what BRI is all about, how it is imperative to biblical stewardship and the opportunity to inspire transformation for God's glory throughout the world. Sally heartily agreed with everything, nodding throughout the education process, vocalizing her support for the pro-life movement and disdain for pornography, human trafficking and other issues.

Sally made statements like, "Wow, this is so wonderful. I can't believe I never heard about this before. This makes total sense!" and excitedly handed over her current investment statement so that I could provide a screening analysis on her current holdings.

This is where things got interesting. On Sally's second appointment, we reviewed the screening analysis of her portfolio which was at a different firm. Her portfolio was like many other investors' portfolios. She owned a few mutual funds, some individual stocks, some better performing than others, and through it all we saw the typical violations: abortion drugs, pornography distribution, alcohol, human rights violations, and the list went on.

When I educate investors on what is going on from a moral perspective in their portfolios, I am always careful to keep the conversation and data very objective and educationally focused, and as far from finger pointing and guilt tripping as humanly possible. My role is not to create guilt and shame, but to educate and offer a path to fix a problem that the investor did not know was there.

Here is what happened with Sally. Everything went just as I would expect from our first meeting together. Sally expressed her concern, shock and dismay that all of these egregious issues were present in her portfolio and made mention of how she wanted to clean things up and invest biblically.

But.

Then we came to the report on one of the stocks that she held. This particular stock had been handed down to her from her grandmother, and was a stock that her grandfather originally purchased almost one hundred years ago. All of the grandkids had inherited shares of this company, and it was sort of a part of their family history since grandma and grandpa were such loyal investors and put all of their investment into that one company, and had done very well since the early 1900's when it was originally purchased.

The problem was, this company was now a major advocate for all sorts of unbiblical activities that deeply contradicted Sally's biblical convictions and conscience as she had expressed very clearly in our two meetings. The report was several pages long with dozens of violations.
Can you guess what Sally's decision was with this stock? All of a sudden, when the abstract idea of excluding companies involved in immoral activities became a concrete issue, and specifically a concrete issue with this specific stock, Sally's convictions were dulled. She began to fish about for justifications to the immoral activities of this company and became defensive about the data being presented about her pet stock.

Ultimately, Sally decided to sell her entire portfolio and

invest biblically responsibly – except for that one stock. Sally's treasure was that stock, her heart was drawn away from her biblical convictions and it caused her to compromise.

Sally could be any number of investors I have met over the years. The story is always the same, only the name of the stock, the reason behind the treasuring and other details are different.

I have a lot of compassion for Sally and others like her. I know how difficult it can be to tear down the idols of our heart. And the Lord knows I have compromised my own biblical convictions more times than I care to remember.

Thank God for his grace and forgiveness that is ours through faith in Christ! I am lost without it.

Investing as worship

This is where biblically responsible investing can also help us in our worship of God. As you align your investments – your literal treasure – with the biblical values that honor and please God, your heart is naturally drawn toward those values as well. This accomplishes two things: First, it tears down any idols that might have been hanging out in your investment portfolio; and second, it directs your heart toward God in worship.

As you go about managing your investment portfolio, keep a close watch over your soul. Discern your motives and ask God for a pure heart that seeks first His kingdom

BIBLICALLY RESPONSIBLE INVESTING

and His righteousness. It doesn't matter if you have $50 thousand or $50 million in your account, your heart is "deceitful above all things" (Jeremiah 17:9) just like mine and we can turn one copper penny into an idol just as easily as the Israelites turned gold into a calf.

So, my dearest rich people, set your hopes on God. Be rich in good works. Share. Store up eternal treasure in heaven. Take hold of that which is truly life.

God help us.

Chapter 10

Risky Business

One of the financial advantages of biblically responsible investing is the opportunity it offers investors to potentially avoid investment risks related to ethical issues. Many investors have been hurt by the collapse of a company in their portfolio that was a result of scandal, moral failures, lack of integrity or other issues addressed by biblically responsible screening of environmental, social and governance (ESG) issues.

Here is a chart with data sourced from Bloomberg with some sobering statistics of stock price returns one year following a major ESG related "risk event". This is a big deal.

DISPLAY 2
Stock price performance one year following ESG risk event

ESG RISK EVENT	DATE	1 YEAR (%)
Energy accounting scandal	8/14/01	-99.6
Telecommunications accounting scandal	3/11/02	-98.6
Upper Big Branch Mine explosion	4/5/10	-52.7
Deepwater Horizon oil spill	4/20/10	-28.2
Automobile airbag recall	1/21/14	-53.5
Pharmaceutical accounting scandal	8/5/15	-91.5
Automobile emissions scandal	9/20/15	-26.4
Average loss to shareholders after 1 year		**-64.4**

Source: Bloomberg. Data as of November 30, 2016. **Past performance is no guarantee of future results.**

Anybody want a piece of that action? I didn't think so. Let's take a look at two other notable examples of stock wipeouts with ethical underpinnings.

Investors burned by tobacco stocks

"Big tobacco" company Philip Morris' stock registered its biggest drop in a decade, plummeting 18% on April 19th, 2018. The sharp decline came on the back of news that the cigarette giant's newest ploy to hook another generation on nicotine — a heat-not-burn tobacco device they call iQor, which heats a tobacco plug instead of lighting it on fire — fell far short of sales projections.

The new iQor product, and several other new attempts at taking tobacco beyond the cigarette, are being brought to market as the smoking industry finds itself struggling to attract new customers...and as their loyal, longtime customers die by the millions due to lung cancer, heart disease and other smoking-induced diseases.

Global smoking statistics from the World Health Organization are gut-wrenching:

- Tobacco kills up to half of its users.
- Tobacco kills more than 7 million people each year. More than 6 million of those deaths are the result of direct tobacco use while around 890 000 are the result of non-smokers being exposed to second-hand smoke.
- Around 80% of the world's 1.1 billion smokers live in low- and middle-income countries

Investors hooked on tobacco (stocks)

And yet, investors seem to have no qualms about profiting from the death of millions as tobacco stocks remain among the biggest holdings of some of the largest mutual funds and ETFs in the world. A quick survey of the most popular smoke stocks, including Phillip Morris, Altria and Vector Group, show companies like Vanguard, American Funds, SPDRs/State Street, DFA Funds, T. Rowe Price, TIAA CREF, iShares, Fidelity and others as their biggest investors[7]. (You can find out if your mutual fund invests in tobacco stocks for free at www.inspireinsight.com.)

Tobacco stocks wise stewardship?

Some investors justify their investment in tobacco companies with the excuse that excluding them from a portfolio might not be "wise stewardship" because their

---
[7] (www.inspireinsight.com 2018)

returns might suffer.

I'm sorry, but give me a break.

Since when did "wise stewardship" include profiting from the sale of an intentionally addictive product that kills half the people that use it? Do we really care more about our profits than people?

And for Christian investors, we should be very aware that an investment in tobacco companies runs counter to Jesus' command to "love your neighbor as yourself". If you love your neighbor, you don't sell them cigarettes.

Christians quit tobacco stocks

Thankfully, despite tobacco stocks continuing to be embraced by some of the largest mutual funds, ETFs, pension funds and other investors, there are a growing number of investors who are kicking the tobacco stock habit and creating demand for tobacco-free investments. The biblically responsible investing movement is adding to that trend as more and more Christians are realizing that they can align their investments with their biblical values.

And if stock price struggles of big tobacco like this one are any indication, investors might consider making a "wise stewardship" decision and purge their portfolios of tobacco faster than you can strike a match.

Will you kick the habit?

Facebook's $120-billion-dollar bad day

Facebook, the Goliath social media platform, took a historic $120 billion fall on Thursday, July 26th, 2018 winning the top spot for the largest one-day loss of any company's market value ever on record.

Interestingly, this massive 19% wipeout was heavily related to ethical missteps linked to user privacy and data security practices, providing a strong reminder that ethical and moral analysis of a company is not just a feel-good activity, but can help investors identify real, tangible financial risk in an investment.

Scorching Decline And Murky Waters

The scorching decline was sparked by the company's quarterly earnings call where Facebook's CFO detailed decreasing user growth, shrinking profit margins and challenges related to new privacy laws in Europe which were hindering Facebook's growth, engagement and ad revenues in the region.

Facebook's epic evaporation of shareholder value also came on the heels of the bombshell Cambridge Analytica scandal which put CEO Mark Zuckerberg in the hot seat before Congress and shed light on the murky waters of Facebook's privacy and data security practices. That scandal also took a big bite out of Facebook's share value. Translation: robust privacy laws make it harder for Facebook to grow and earn a profit. Food for thought.

Ethics As Risk Management

Companies that stretch the boundaries of ethical business practices, or even outright cross them, may find short-term financial success. But, eventually their chickens come home to roost. Facebook — and everyone who owned Facebook stock — found this out the hard way.

Financial analysts would explain this by saying that corporations which externalize the cost of ethical issues (such as privacy concerns) are by definition over-monetized. Eventually those externalities manifest themselves in the company's balance sheet, the over-monetization is corrected and shareholders pay the price.

The Bible says it this way, "Do not be deceived: God is not mocked, for whatever one sows, that will he also reap." (Galatians 6:7)

Jesus And Financial Advice

Sometimes biblically responsible investors are mocked by the Wall Street establishment as bleeding hearts that focus too much on "soft" or "subjective" issues, instead of the cold hard facts of financial analysis. My question is, if focusing only on financial data is supposedly the highest and best way to invest, why did so many of these investing experts take their share of a $120 billion bath in Facebook stock? Why didn't they see this coming? Why did they get hit by that bus while biblically responsible investors stood safely on the sidewalk?

Because of ethical concerns, such as Facebook's data privacy issues, as well as other moral problems like Facebook's corporate support of abortion and jaw-dropping lack of concern for fighting child pornography which runs rampant on their platform, Facebook stock has been excluded from biblically responsible portfolios.

As biblically responsible investors, we look at both the financial and moral issues related to a potential investment. Only when both areas of analysis are satisfied do we take a position in a stock. As Jesus said, "Be as wise as serpents and innocent as doves." (Matthew 10:16)

As it turns out, this is not only great advice for your spiritual life, but for your financial portfolio as well.

Maybe Wall Street should start reading the Bible.

Chapter 11

Bitcoin Binge: To Byte Or Not To Byte?

Making heads or tails of Bitcoin

And what about investments in more exotic financial instruments?

I just received an email proclaiming that if I started investing in Bitcoin today that I could "make as much as 55 times your money". To which I assume they expect me to respond with something along the lines of, "55 times my money, eh? Well in that case, here is my life savings. Shall I wire it to you? Or do you prefer a suitcase full of cash?"

Maybe you have received similar emails about the phenomenon that is the Bitcoin investment rage du jour.

So, what's up with Bitcoin anyway? Is it actually a thing? Should Bitcoin be a part of your portfolio as an investor? Should Bitcoin be a part of your portfolio as a biblically responsible investor?

If you have no idea what Bitcoin is, I don't blame you. I think most people don't really know what it is — including those who own Bitcoins and possibly even those who are aggressively marketing Bitcoins for investment.

What is Bitcoin?

Bitcoin is the first and most popular "cryptocurrency", which are virtual, computer generated, de-centralized currencies available to anyone who has Internet access. Bitcoin allows you to convert your old-fashioned money (such as US Dollars) into Bitcoins by buying them on an exchange from someone who already owns Bitcoins.

There are numerous Bitcoin exchanges that offer "virtual wallets" which serve as a sort of Bitcoin bank account online, on your computer or on your smartphone. There are even Bitcoin ATMs that have sprung up around the globe to facilitate Bitcoin deposits and withdrawals (hint: no physical Bitcoins go in or out of those machines, they are strictly electronic transfer devices that provide paper receipts). And some bold businesses have begun accepting Bitcoin as payment, and even paying employees and vendors in Bitcoins instead of traditional currency.

If you are really gung-ho, you could even go into the Bitcoin mining business, wherein you purchase specialized computer software and hardware that enables you to run a complicated algorithm in an attempt to "crack the code" and "verify" a Bitcoin transaction. When your computer hits upon the correct code, you are rewarded with 25 Bitcoins for your efforts. Every four years, the number of Bitcoins granted in this "verification reward" is cut in half, reducing the payoff for this activity. Also, the "blockchain" code becomes increasingly complex with each verification, making it increasingly difficult to mine Bitcoins as the remaining coins become more scarce.

Bitcoin miners can continue their hunt for new Bitcoins until the total number of Bitcoins in circulation is 21 million, at which point there are no more Bitcoins left to find. This limitation was built into the Bitcoin blockchain rules at the outset to ensure that there was a limited supply, and thus value relative to demand. The bigger your computing power, the better your chances of successfully mining Bitcoins becomes.

Yes, this is really happening. And no, George Orwell is not the author of Bitcoin.

Bitcoin is big business

On January 1, 2011, $100 US Dollars would have bought you about 333.33 Bitcoins (Bitcoin was valued at 30 cents per coin at that time, according to the CoinDesk Bitcoin Price Index[8]). If you held on to those Bitcoins through the hyper-volatile roller coaster of price swings that has defined Bitcoin value since inception, on December

---
[8] (www.coindesk.com 2018)

31st, 2017 your Bitcoins would have been worth about $4,600,154.00 US Dollars (Bitcoin value $13,800.60 USD per coin[9]).

Of course, just a few months later, Bitcoin prices continued on their eccentric way and as of September 11, 2018 prices were half of what they were nine months earlier[10].

Wow. No wonder there is so much media noise about Bitcoin speculation.

Should Christians invest in Bitcoin?

No doubt the astronomical price returns on Bitcoin over the past years is very tempting to investors everywhere. I mean, who wouldn't like to turn $100 into over four million dollars in just a few years?

Let me say that again. This time let it really sink in… $100 into over four million dollars in just a few years.
Does anybody else hear warning bells in that sentence, or is it just me?

Well, King Solomon might have something to say about that. After all, he was the one who wrote, "Wealth gained hastily will dwindle, but whoever gathers little by little will increase it" (Proverbs 13:11).

And the Apostle Paul would have a few thoughts on the matter as well as he wrote, "But those who desire to be

---
[9] (www.CoinDesk.com 2018)
[10] (www.coindesk.com 2018)

rich fall into temptation, into a snare, into many senseless and harmful desires that plunge people into ruin and destruction" (1 Timothy 6:9-10).

If I had to guess at the primary motivation that drives people to exchange their actual money for Bitcoins, I would say that it is greed, plain and simple. The desire to be rich. The desire to be rich fast. The desire to be rich easily.

Greed is never a good reason to do anything. If you are considering buying into Bitcoin, first check your heart and be honest about what your motivation is for doing so. Is it greed? Then don't do it.

Besides, when anything goes up in value that far, that fast I can only think of tech stocks in 2001 and financial stocks in 2008. Also tulip bulbs in 1630. When will the Bitcoin bubble burst? I don't know, but it is coming and I don't want any part of it.

The dark side of Bitcoin

Aside from the problems of greed and bubbles waiting to burst, there is a very real, very insidious side to Bitcoin that Christian investors should think about very carefully. It is becoming increasingly evident that ISIS and other terror groups are exploiting Bitcoin to fund their massive budgets and evil purposes. In 2017, a woman was arrested and charged with laundering $85,000 through Bitcoin and other cryptocurrencies to the Islamic State.

Zoobiah Shahnaz, age 27 from Long Island, allegedly used 16 credit cards (which she had obtained by fraudulent methods) to purchase $63,000 in Bitcoin and other cryptocurrencies, in addition to $22,500 she was able to acquire through a loan from a Manhattan bank. Shahnaz was detained by federal agents at JFK International Airport as she was attempting to board a flight to Syria to join ISIS in person.

And she is not the only one.

In fact, a prominent pro-ISIS blog which is used to recruit and train terrorists, explains to readers how Bitcoins can be used to fund the Islamic State's detestable activities without being traced by Western "Kafir" governments. God only knows how much of the hundreds of billions of dollars currently in Bitcoin is supporting the most blatantly evil organizations on the face of the planet.

Of course, terrorists can use any kind of currency to fund their atrocities. But Bitcoin is designed with the specific purpose of being completely anonymous, untraceable and detached from any government or law enforcement protections. The black market loves Bitcoin.

Bitcoin may be the closest thing to blood money the world has ever seen.

Bitcoin or bust?

Listen, you are not evil if you buy some Bitcoins. Unless you are a member of ISIS and then, yes, you are evil.

(And if we are talking theology of total depravity here, then we understand that you and I are actually evil even if we don't own Bitcoin, which is why we are in such a need for a Savior to redeem us from the pit!)

Regardless, there are significant problems with the Bitcoin economy that any wise investor must take into consideration before jumping into that dark pool. Allow me to summarize them here:

- Bitcoin is very weird. You probably don't understand what you are buying.
- You probably want to buy Bitcoin because of the lure of fast, easy riches. That is greed.
- Bitcoin values have skyrocketed to ridiculously astronomical heights in a ridiculously short amount of time. Usually, that means something has got to give. And usually that means the bubble is ripe for the popping.
- Bitcoin is perhaps the bad guys' favorite thing in the world and is funding the most despicable acts of evil the world has seen in a very long time, all with complete anonymity and without the pesky oversight of law enforcement.

For all of these reasons, you can count me out of the Bitcoin binge. How about you?

Chapter 12

Start

My hope is that within the pages of this book you have seen that there truly is a movement underway in the world of finance. Christians are investing billions of dollars intentionally to support biblical values for the glory of God, and it is called biblically responsible investing. More and more Christians are waking up to the opportunity to align their investments with biblical values, as well as discovering the unsettling truth that they have previously been profiting from immoral businesses such as abortion, pornography, human trafficking and other unbiblical practices.

The growing demand for biblically responsible investments is changing the landscape of Wall Street and gaining global recognition as a powerful force for positive change for God's glory throughout the world. However, many

Christian investors are at a loss for how to get started with biblically responsible investing, but biblically responsible investing does not have to be complicated. This chapter is meant to give you a simple road map to follow so you can join the ranks of biblically responsible investors who are investing for God's glory and their joy.

The end of a book may be an odd place for a chapter titled "Start", but in one sense that is the most appropriate placement. "For if anyone is a hearer of the word and not a doer, he is like a man who looks intently at his natural face in a mirror. For he looks at himself and goes away and at once forgets what he was like. But the one who looks into the perfect law, the law of liberty, and perseveres, being no hearer who forgets but a doer who acts, he will be blessed in his doing" (James 1:23-25).

Be a doer, not just a hearer. Do not let the sun sink tonight before you take your first steps into the BRI movement. Do not let the fire die down before you throw more logs onto the blaze. Respond in faith to the word of God that teaches us all to glorify Him in everything we do and with everything He has given us.

Become a biblically responsible investor today, for God's glory and your joy.

Following is a step by step guide to make it simple and easy to implement biblically responsible investing in your financial life.

Step 1: Discover What You Own From A Biblically Responsible Investing Perspective

The first step in the journey towards biblically responsible investing is to discover the truth about what you own in your investment account. What are the companies that you own in your 401(k), IRA, mutual funds, ETFs and other investments doing to turn a profit? Are they manufacturing abortion drugs, selling pornography, using slave labor in their supply chains? Are they donating money to Planned Parenthood? Lobbying to advance the LGBT agenda? I vividly remember the moment that I discovered the troubling truth of what I was invested in and how shocked I was to find that here I was, the president of our local pro-life pregnancy center, and I also owned stock in 3 companies through my mutual funds that were manufacturing abortion drugs. That means that every time a young woman went to Planned Parenthood and had an abortion, I was profiting from that transaction. That realization changed my life forever, as it has for countless other biblically responsible investors around the world today.

So, how do you go about finding out what the moral value of your portfolio is? It is certainly a daunting task to consider, and quite impossible for the average investor to compile the amount of research necessary to dig into the dirty details of every company in their portfolio. After all, it is hard enough just to read your quarterly statement without going cross eyed, let alone pour through thousands of hard to find data points on thousands of publicly traded companies.

The good news is that you don't have to because there are Christian financial professionals, such as the members of our Christian Wealth Management network, that have robust analytic technology where they plug in your investment ticker symbols and out pops easy to understand reports that show you everything you ever wanted to know (and everything you NEVER wanted to know) about the moral issues in your portfolio.

There is also www.inspireinsight.com, which is a free online tool that our team built to empower investors with the biblical values data they need to make informed, God honoring decisions. Insight brings together the most robust data sets from the world's leading providers, such as Thomson Reuters, Value Line, TruValue Labs and others, and makes that information freely available to anyone with an Internet connection.

All you need is to type in your ticker symbols or search the name of a company and instantly you have all the data related to the biblical values issues, both good and bad, that company is involved in as well as financial performance data so that you can make an investment decision that is both "wise as a serpent and innocent as a dove" (Matthew 10:16).

Are you ready to discover the truth about your investments? Ignorance is certainly not bliss, and I encourage you to take that step and see for yourself what is going on behind closed doors in your portfolio.

Step 2: Explore Biblically Responsible Investing Options

If you are like me, once you discover the moral issues in your current portfolio you will want to make a change as soon as possible. So, how do you build a biblically responsible investing portfolio? Upon learning about biblically responsible investing, some Christian investors have the concern that it will be difficult to find enough quality biblically responsible investment options to construct an outstanding portfolio that meets their financial goals. But praise God that the fact of the matter is that the overwhelming majority of companies pass even the most stringent biblically responsible investing screening criterion so that there is no shortage of quality companies for biblically responsible investors to allocate capital to. There are also a large and growing number of biblically responsible investing mutual funds, including lower cost ETFs (exchange traded funds) and other professionally managed investment vehicles available for biblically responsible investors and Christian financial advisors to use in their portfolios.

One word of caution: there are many investment funds issued by Christian faith-based organizations that one would assume are managed according to biblically responsible investing guidelines, but in fact do very little (or sometimes zero) investment screening. Also, not every Christian financial advisor is trained or equipped in biblically responsible investing, so do not just assume because your advisor is a Christian that they are managing your investments according to biblical values. Many Christian advisors, just like Christian investors, still have no idea that there is a major moral dilemma present in the portfolios they manage. As a good steward of God's investments, be sure to do your homework and check the biblically responsible investing reports on www.inspireinsight.com even for Christian funds and advisors to make sure you know what you are investing in.

Once you identify your available investment options that meet biblically responsible investing screening criterion, the rest of the investment selection process is exactly the same as building any other portfolio: consider the risks, returns, fees, diversification and other important aspects to build your biblically responsible investing portfolio.

If you are a do-it-yourself investor, you can find many helpful resources direct from investment fund providers and analysis sites like www.inspireinsight.com. If managing your own investment portfolio is not on your list of favorite things to do, consider working with a Christian financial advisor who is trained in biblically responsible investing, like our Christian Wealth Management professional network members.

Step 3: Start Biblically Responsible Investing And Impact The World For God's Glory!

After discovering what you own from a biblically responsible investing perspective, and then exploring your biblically responsible investing options, it is time to pull the proverbial trigger and become a biblically responsible investor, joining the growing number of other Christian investors in the biblically responsible investing movement!

The BRI movement is an exciting phenomenon that Wall Street is completely unprepared for. I have spoken with thousands of Christian investors and advisors over the past several years and I can attest to the fact that there is an awakening going on where the Holy Spirit is illuminating the importance of investing for God's glory and placing a passionate conviction in the hearts of His people zealous to honor God in their financial life, just as they do in other areas of life.

God makes it clear in His word, the Holy Bible, that He wants His people to manage His money according to His values for His glory, and our joy. "So whether you eat or drink, or whatever you do, do all to the glory of God" (1 Corinthians 10:31). Christians control trillions of dollars in investment assets[11], [12], and together we can inspire transformation for God's glory throughout the world by aligning our investments (God's investments!) with biblical values, sending a powerful message to Wall Street and corporations everywhere that God's people care about biblical values enough to "put our money where our faith is".

There are already biblically responsible investing success stories, such as corporations ending their philanthropic support of Planned Parenthood and hotels removing pornography from their televisions, and by the grace of God we will see even more of these inspiring stories unfolding. But, even if nothing changes and corporations continue to go from bad to worse, it is still the biblically

---

[11] (www.epi.org/publication/retirement-in-america/#charts 2018)
[12] (http://www.pewforum.org/religious-landscape-study/ 2018)

responsible investor's joy to glorify God by honoring His values with His investment assets. One day we will all stand before our Lord and give an account for what we have done with all He has given us during our time on earth. I want to hear the "well done, good and faithful servant. Enter into the joy of your master" regarding every part of my life, including how I managed God's investments.

What about you?

Appendix:

Critical Considerations When Looking For A Christian Financial Advisor

Some investors are independent do-it-yourselfers and enjoy watching over their own portfolio. They feel confident in their ability to successfully manage their nest egg through the ups and downs of the stock market and have the time to devote in order to do a proper job of it.

But many investors feel ill-prepared to make proper investment management decisions, when to sell or not to sell, what to buy, how to analyze an investment against another.

And still more investors recognize that, although they have the education and know-how to invest on their own, there is one thing that they are incapable of managing on their own: their emotions. Outside counsel is valuable because sometimes we just don't know what we don't know or we can't see through our own assumptions because we have only one perspective. There is a reason that King Solomon encouraged counsel, "Where there is no guidance a people falls, but in an abundance of counselors there is safety" (Proverbs 11:14).

If you are an investor who desires to receive wise, biblically sound financial advice, there are some important considerations to remember in your search for the right advisor. Following is a discussion of how to successfully find an advisor who can guide you with a biblical perspective to glorify God in your financial life.

How Do You Find A Christian Financial Advisor?

How do you find a Christian financial advisor? It can be a stressful process. Who can you trust to skillfully and wisely guide you through all of life's financial twists and turns? What if you find a Christian financial advisor and they end up being the wrong pick? And what if you don't realize they are the wrong advisor until it is too late? And for us Christians, are there biblical considerations that we should take into account to find a financial advisor?

Here are four qualities that Christian investors should demand when looking to find a financial advisor.

Find A Christian Financial Advisor Who Fears The Lord

If you want a financial advisor who has wisdom, then this is a non-negotiable. The Bible says, "The fear of the Lord is the beginning of wisdom, and the knowledge of the

Holy One is insight" (Proverbs 9:10). If we are to believe the Bible, which we do, then this verse states very plainly that only those who fear the Lord can attain to wisdom. If the fear of the Lord is the beginning of wisdom, and a certain financial advisor does not fear the Lord, then scripture says that financial advisor does not have wisdom. But some may challenge this notion, asking, "Surely there are non-Christian financial advisors who give good advice, aren't there?"

To answer that question, let's start by assuming that the Bible is actually correct, which it is. Next, let us consider the definition of "wisdom". Does wisdom mean making decisions or giving advice that has beneficial earthly outcomes, such as a high performing investment portfolio? Or is there a deeper, and more important element to wisdom that the Bible is referring to?

Consider another verse of scripture dealing with wisdom, "For the wisdom of this world is folly with God. For it is written, 'He catches the wise in their craftiness,' and again, 'The Lord knows the thoughts of the wise, that they are futile'" (1 Corinthians 3:19-20). This verse makes clear that God has a different definition of wisdom than the world does — and importantly, His definition is the correct definition!

True wisdom has its roots in the fear of the Lord, and as such it always brings glory to God. Worldly "wisdom" has its roots in the cleverness of men, and as such never brings glory to God. We must recognize that there are decisions that the world would count as wise but that are complete foolishness to God. Conversely, there are decisions that God counts as wise, yet the world sees as abject folly.

Which decisions would you rather make?

Find A Christian Financial Advisor Who Operates With Excellence

But, that does not mean that all Christian financial advisors give wise advice.
That brings us to the second point. At the risk of sounding redundant, if a Christian investor is going to seek advice from a financial advisor, they should only seek advice from a Christian financial advisor. Always.

And they should also demand excellence from that Christian financial advisor, just as they would from any other professional advising them on the most important decisions in their life. Always.

Scripture warns believers about receiving advice from those who are not following after Christ:

"Blessed is the man
   who walks not in the counsel of the wicked,
nor stands in the way of sinners,
   nor sits in the seat of scoffers;
but his delight is in the law of the Lord,
   and on his law he meditates day and night"
(Psalm 1:1-2).

We must remind ourselves that apart from Christ, "None

is righteous, no not one" (Romans 3:10). Only by grace through faith in Christ can we escape our wicked, sinful, scoffing state of depravity. "And because of him you are in Christ Jesus, who became to us wisdom from God, righteousness and sanctification and redemption, so that, as it is written, 'Let the one who boasts, boast in the Lord'" (1 Corinthians 1:30-31).

The implication is that no matter how nice, talented or helpful an unbelieving financial advisor is, they have not had their minds, hearts and spirits renewed by faith in Christ, and as such their advice is inherently, spiritually flawed and the Bible warns us not to seek their guidance, not to "walk in their counsel".

However, that does not mean that Christian investors should choose to work with just any Christian financial advisor. Putting a Jesus fish on a business card is not a free pass to deliver sub-standard performance. "Whatever you do, work heartily, as for the Lord and not for men…You are serving the Lord Christ" (Colossians 3:23-24).

Christian professionals should be the hardest working, most trustworthy, devoted to excellence individuals in the marketplace. Christian investors should demand excellence in their search to find a Christian financial advisor.

Find A Christian Financial Advisor With Godly Character

Jesus said, "Each tree is known by its own fruit" (Luke 6:44).

There are many people who may claim the name of "Christian", yet their pattern of life does not give evidence of the Lordship of Christ. Put another way, there are many financial advisors who may claim the name of "Christian", yet there is no "fruit" to give us confidence that they are born again followers of Christ.

Worse than that, there are also those who would masquerade under the Christian banner with the explicit purpose of defrauding Christian investors. Wolves in sheep's clothing.

Before doing business with a Christian financial advisor, be sure to evaluate their character and pattern of life. Check character references from a pastor, ask them what church they attend and what ministries they serve or volunteer in.

Only God truly knows the heart, but the Bible exhorts us to be wise in our assessment of the people in our life, and especially those who we take advice from.

Find A Christian Financial Advisor Skilled In Biblically Responsible Investing

Finally, Christian investors should look for a Christian financial advisor who is skilled in biblically responsible investing.

BRI is the practice of aligning investment portfolios to support biblical values by excluding companies that are engaged in immoral activities, such as abortion or human trafficking, and instead seeking to invest in companies which are more closely aligned with God's heart and operate as a blessing to the world.

Unfortunately, many Christian financial advisors do not have the resources or experience to deliver high quality, biblically responsible investing advice. Often this is no fault of the advisor, but rather a result of their firm not having a robust lineup of biblically responsible investing offerings. And sometimes the advisor may have the investments available for his or her use, but lack experience in managing a quality BRI portfolio that rivals or exceeds the results one would expect from a worthwhile investment.

Thankfully, there are a growing number of biblically responsible investing options becoming available to Christian financial advisors at firms across the nation. And there is also a growing knowledge bank of best practices, training, screening technology and other professional resources becoming available to equip Christian financial advisors to become proficient in providing biblically responsible investing services.

The largest multi-firm, nationwide membership network of Christian financial advisors dedicated specifically to advancing the BRI movement is Christian Wealth Management. Full disclosure, I am also the founder and CEO of Christian Wealth Management, so I might be a little biased in saying that www.ChristianWealthManagement.com could be a great place to start for investors looking to find a Christian financial advisor to provide them with sophisticated guidance from a biblical perspective. I recommend you visit the site and judge for yourself.

All For God's Glory

There are many important considerations when choosing a financial advisor, and for Christian investors there are additional qualities in the areas of godly character, fear of the Lord, God-glorifying excellence and biblically responsible investing which must be examined. Find a Christian financial advisor who displays all of these traits, and you have found an advisor who is worth listening to.

Scripture compels us to live our entire lives for the glory of God, and the management of our finances (which ultimately belong to God) is no exception. Don't settle for anything less.

References

Enete, Shane. 2018. How Negative Ethical Screening According to Evangelical Christian Principles Influences Stock Returns. Brea, CA: Biola University.

2018. http://www.pewforum.org/religious-landscape-study/. September 20. Accessed September 20, 2018.

Moyer, Liz. 2017. "Funds Invoke Bible Values, Others See Intolerance." The New York Times, February 28: 1

Oxford University and Arabesque Partners. 2015. From The Stockholder To The Stakeholder: How Sustainability Can Drive Financial Outperformance. Oxford University and Arabesque Partners. Accessed 9 11, 2018. https://arabesque.com/research/From_the_stockholder_to_the_stakeholder_web.pdf.

Ritholtz, Barry. 2017. Thou Shalt Not Buy Biblically Responsible ETFs. New York, NY, March 2.

Wharton School of Business: University of Pennsylvania. 2015. Great Expectations:

Mission Preservation and Financial Performance in Impact Investing. Research Report, Philadelphia, PA: Wharton School of Business.

2018. www.coindesk.com. September 20. Accessed September 20, 2018. https://www.coindesk.com/price/.

2018. www.epi.org/publication/retirement-in-america/#charts. September 20. Accessed September 20, 2018. https://www.epi.org/publication/retirement-in-america/#charts.

2018. www.inspireinsight.com. September 20. Accessed September 20, 2018. www.inspireinsight.com.

Advisory services are offered through CWM Advisors, LLC. dba Inspire, a Registered Investment Adviser with the SEC.